W9-AJT-055

DATE DUE

JA 3 '89	AY 30 '04	
AP 7 '89	SEP 29 '01	
JY 12 '89	FEB 31 '09	
	DEC 23	
AG 25 '89	JY 09 '02	
MR 16 '90	MR 25 '03	
OC 23 '91	NO 06 '03	
OF 6 '91		
OC 15 '92		
OC 4 '93		
MAR 4 '90		
JUN 22 '94		

523.1
Asi

Asimov, Isaac
How was the universe
born?

ISAAC ASIMOV'S
Library of the Universe

How Was the Universe Born?

by Isaac Asimov

Gareth Stevens Publishing
Milwaukee

1/30/08 4quia Source 8.24

80077

The reproduction rights to all photographs and illustrations in this book are controlled by the individuals or institutions credited on page 32 and may not be reproduced without their permission.

Library of Congress Cataloging-in-Publication Data

Asimov, Isaac, 1920-
　　How was the universe born?

　　(Isaac Asimov's Library of the universe)
　　Bibliography: p.
　　Includes index.
　　Summary: Discusses the origins and characteristics of our universe, focusing on the nature of stars.
　　1. Cosmology -- Juvenile literature. [1. Cosmology. 2. Universe. 3. Stars.
I. Title. II. Series: Asimov, Isaac, 1920-　　. Library of the Universe.
QB983.A86　1988　　523.1　　87-42602
ISBN 1-55532-383-9
ISBN 1-55532-358-8 (lib. bdg.)

A Gareth Stevens Children's Books edition.

Edited, designed, and produced by
Gareth Stevens, Inc.　7317 West Green Tree Road Milwaukee, Wisconsin 53223, USA

Text copyright © 1989 by Nightfall, Inc.
End matter copyright © 1989 by Gareth Stevens, Inc. and Martin Greenberg
Format copyright © 1989 by Gareth Stevens, Inc.

First published in the United States and Canada in 1989 by Gareth Stevens, Inc.
All rights reserved. No part of this book may be reproduced or utilized in any form or by any means without permission in writing from Gareth Stevens, Inc.

Cover painting © Julian Baum
Designer: Laurie Shock
Picture research: Kathy Keller
Artwork commissioning: Kathy Keller and Laurie Shock
Project editor: Mark Sachner
Research editor: Scott Enk
Technical advisers and consulting editors: Greg Walz-Chojnacki and Francis Reddy

1 2 3 4 5 6 7 8 9 94 93 92 91 90 89

CONTENTS

Nowadays, we have seen planets up close, all the way to distant Uranus. We have mapped Venus through its clouds. We have seen dead volcanoes on Mars and live ones on Io, one of Jupiter's moons. We have put spacecraft with measuring devices on the surfaces of Mars and Venus. Human beings have even walked on our Moon!

But the greatest drama of all is to try to understand the Universe as a whole. We can only begin to try to grasp its vastness and to study all the strange things we find in it. Some of these things — quasars, pulsars, and black holes — we didn't even dream of until the last few decades.

So let's learn a bit about the amazing story of our Universe!

Isaac Asimov

Above: According to ancient Greek myths, the god Helios drove the chariot that carries the Sun across the sky.

Left: Nut, a sky goddess of ancient Egypt.

Right: The stars of summer gleam like jewels on the dome of the night sky.

Primitive Ideas

Long ago, human beings could only suppose that the Universe was what it looked like to them.

The Earth? It seemed to be no more than a round patch of flat ground, not very big. The sky? It seemed to be a solid dome that came down to meet the ground all around, at places not far off. The Sun? It traveled across the sky to give us light and warmth. The sky was blue when the Sun was present, but turned black when it set. In the night sky, there were many, many specks of light — stars — in the dome of the sky. The Moon, which went through a change of shape every month, moved among the stars. A few stars were brighter than the others, and they also moved.

Where Is Earth?

The ancient Greeks said that Earth was a large sphere and thought it was at the center of the Universe. They thought that the Moon circled around the Earth. Outside the Moon's orbit circled Mercury, Venus, the Sun, Mars, Jupiter, and Saturn. Outside the orbits of all these bodies were the sky and the stars.

In 1543, Copernicus (pronounced co-PER-nic-us) showed that it made more sense to suppose that the Sun was at the center, and that all the planets moved around it. Earth was one of the planets, and it went around the Sun, too. Beyond that were the stars, but they weren't attached to the sky. Later, Edmund Halley found out that the stars moved, too.

Did the death of a star cause the birth of _our_ star?

The Solar system formed from a gigantic cloud of dust and gas a little less than five billion years ago. That cloud of dust and gas must have existed all through the life of the Universe. So it was perhaps 10 to 15 billion years old when it began to collapse to form the Sun and planets. Why did it suddenly start to collapse after all that time? Astronomers think that the shock of a nearby exploding star called a supernova might have started the cloud's collapse. But they still aren't _sure_ that that's what happened.

Left: Nicolaus Copernicus — the Polish philosopher, doctor, and astronomer who showed that the planets circle the Sun.

Lower left: the Copernican system. The Sun lies in the center and Earth circles around it.

Below: Star trails in a time-exposure photo of the night sky. From where we stand on Earth, the Sun, Moon, planets, and stars all seem to wheel across the sky — small wonder people once thought Earth was the center of the Universe!

Island Universes

In 1785, William Herschel (HER-shell) showed that all the stars formed a large collection shaped like a lens. We call this collection the Milky Way Galaxy. This is our Galaxy, and it is 100,000 light-years across. Each light-year is almost six trillion miles (9.5 trillion km) long.

There are other galaxies as well. They look like cloudy patches in the sky, but they are really other galaxies very far away. The closest large galaxy is the Andromeda Galaxy, which is over two million light-years away. Many other galaxies are scattered through space. There might be a hundred billion in all!

The German-born English astronomer William Herschel, discoverer of the planet Uranus. He designed the best telescopes of his time.

If we could view our Milky Way from the outside, it would look like the Great Galaxy in Andromeda, seen here without the aid of a telescope.

Right: Through a telescope, ragged dust clouds appear around the Andromeda Galaxy's core. Over two million light-years away, it's the closest galaxy that resembles our own spiral, the Milky Way. (The white streak across the sky is the light reflected off an artificial satellite moving overhead.)

The Red Shift

In 1842, Christian Doppler explained why anything noisy sounds more shrill when it comes toward you, and sounds deeper when it goes away from you. A similar kind of change, or shift, happens with light.

Austrian scientist Christian Doppler.

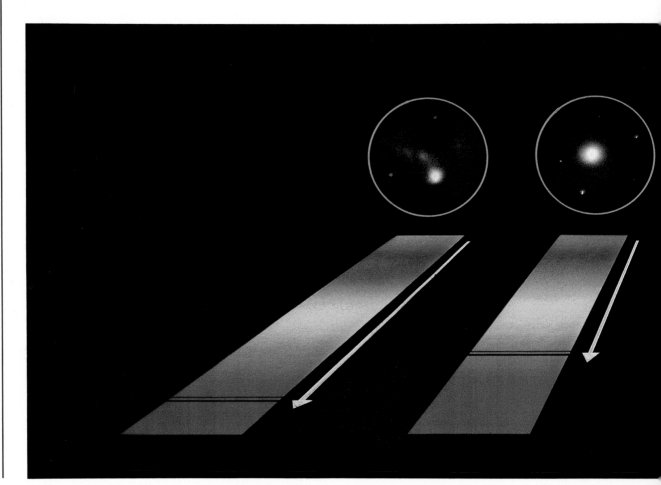

Every star sends out light waves. The light appears bluer if the star is coming toward us, and redder if it is moving away. In the 1920s, astronomers found that most galaxies show a "red shift." This means that they are moving away from our Galaxy. The farther away they are, the faster they move away from us. The farthest galaxies are moving away at thousands of miles a second!

When light from a star or galaxy is spread out into a rainbow of color, dark lines show up where light has been absorbed by the atoms of that star or galaxy. The lines in the light of distant galaxies are shifted toward ever redder light as we look farther away.

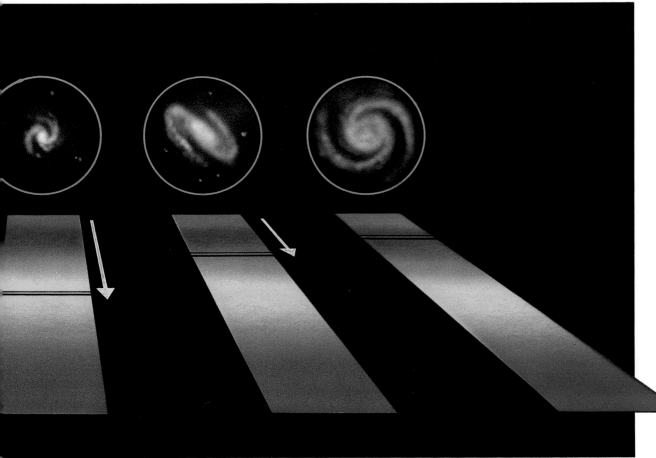

The Outer Limits

The most distant galaxies we can see are hundreds of millions of light-years away. In the 1950s, astronomers discovered certain galaxies that sent out radio waves. These galaxies were studied carefully, and the light waves they sent out looked very strange. In 1963, astronomers found that this was because the light waves were very stretched out.

Galaxies like this are called quasars. Quasars had the largest red shifts known, so they must be very far away. Even the closest quasars are a billion light-years away. One quasar discovered recently is 12 billion light-years away! So when we look at quasars, we are looking back into a time before our Sun was born!

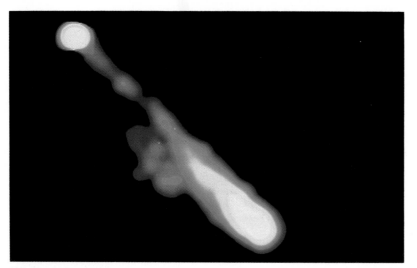

Radio telescopes created this image of a huge gas jet erupting from quasar 3C 273. The jet is a million light-years long!

Right: Appearances can be deceiving. A bridge of gas seems to connect a quasar (top) to a much closer galaxy (below). Astronomers believe that such connections are optical illusions. Colors are added to the picture to bring out faint details.

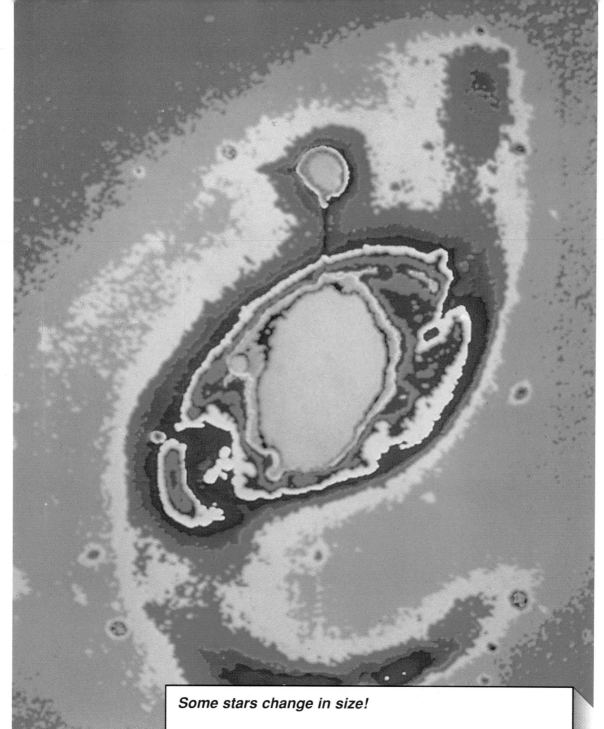

Some stars change in size!

Some stars grow larger and smaller in a regular rhythm. We say that they pulsate. Pulsating stars are called variable stars. The larger and brighter pulsating stars are, the more slowly they pulse. We can tell how bright they really are from how quickly or slowly they pulse. And we can tell how far away they are from how bright they seem to be. Scientists have used variable stars in nearby galaxies to find out how far away the galaxies are.

The Universe — It's a Big Place!

The known planets orbit the Sun in a region only about seven billion miles (11 billion km) in diameter. That's just a little over a thousandth of a light-year. The nearest star is 4.2 light-years away. That's thousands of times as far away as the farthest planet in our Solar system.

The farthest stars in our Galaxy are 100,000 light-years away. The Andromeda Galaxy is over two million light-years away,

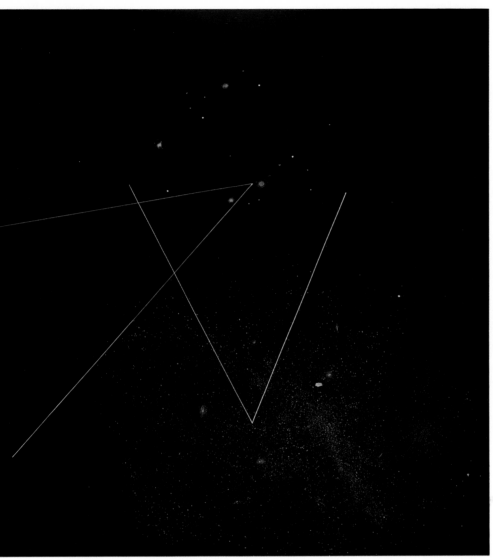

We think of Earth as quite big, but this painting puts us in our place! From left to right, we see that Earth is just one of nine worlds orbiting the Sun. Our Sun itself is just one of 200 billion stars in the Milky Way Galaxy. The Milky Way is but one of many galaxies in our cluster, and one of <u>billions</u> of galaxies in the Universe.

but it's our next-door neighbor. The farthest known quasar is about 12 billion light-years away.

In all the Universe, there are about 100 billion galaxies. And each galaxy contains about 100 billion stars.

Imagine how small our own Earth is in comparison!

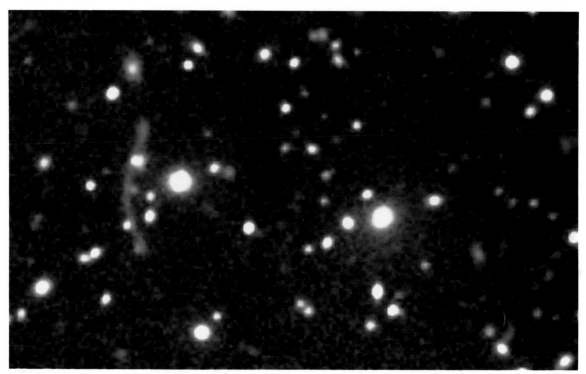

A galaxy cluster. The glowing arcs in this picture might be formed by light pulled off course by a tremendous but unidentified source of gravity. No one knows for sure.

The Expanding Universe

Why are all the galaxies moving away from us? Why should the galaxies farthest away from us move away the fastest? What's so special about us?

The answer is that it isn't us at all! Galaxies exist in groups called clusters. Every cluster moves away from every other cluster. No matter what cluster we might live in, the others would be moving away from us. The Universe is always expanding — growing larger. The space between galaxies is getting bigger. But scientists didn't know this until 1929.

Why is the Universe like soap bubbles?

Throughout the Universe, galaxies seem to form lines and even curves. They enclose large spaces in which there seems to be very little matter. If we could look at the Universe from a great distance and see it all at once, we would think it looked like soap bubbles. Galaxies would be like the soap film making up the bubbles. The bubbles themselves would be empty and come in different sizes. Astronomers still don't know why the galaxies were formed in this way.

"Soap bubble" galaxies.

The Big Bang

The Universe is expanding as time goes on. But suppose we look backward in time.

As we go farther and farther back in time, the galaxies move closer and closer together. If we went back in time far enough, all the galaxies would crunch together into a small space.

That was the way it was in the beginning. The whole thing must have exploded in a "Big Bang." The Universe is still expanding as a result of that Big Bang. If we measure how fast the Universe is expanding and how long it must have taken to reach its present size, we know that the Big Bang happened 15 to 20 billion years ago.

> *Okay — but what came <u>before</u> the Big Bang?*
>
> *As scientists try to figure out the history of the Universe, they reach a point where the laws of science don't seem to work. They can only describe the Universe a fraction of a second after the Big Bang. But what existed <u>before</u> the birth of the Universe? One scientist thinks the cosmos might have been born from <u>nothing</u>. But no one can really say!*

Imagine that galaxies are like the raisins in raisin bread dough. The raisins start off fairly close together (top). If you could stand on any one of them as the dough expands (bottom), all the other raisins would appear to be moving away from you. As space expands, all the galaxies appear to be moving away from us.

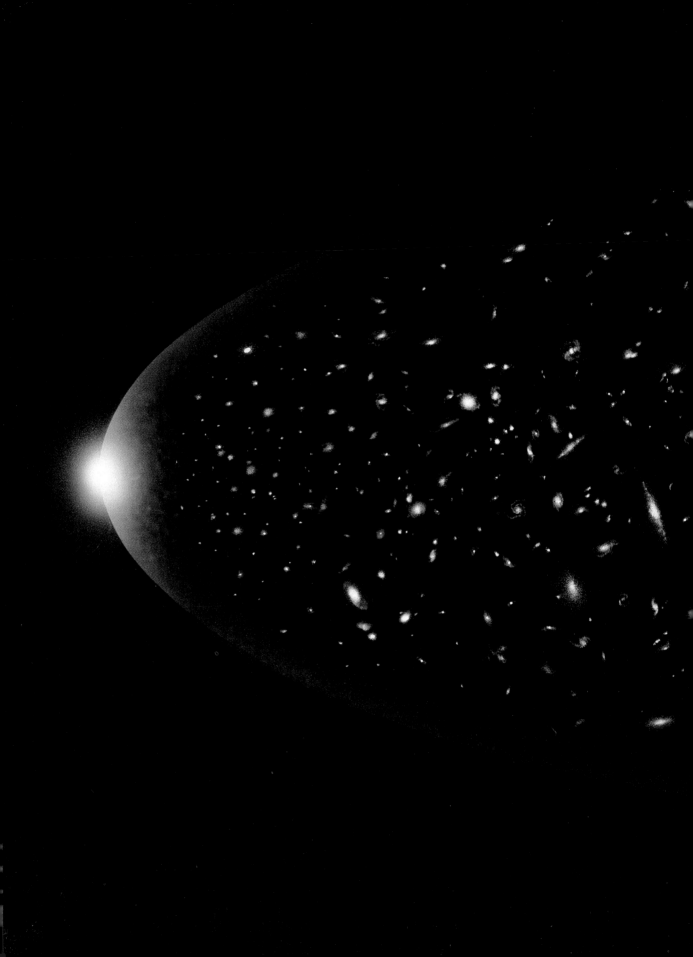

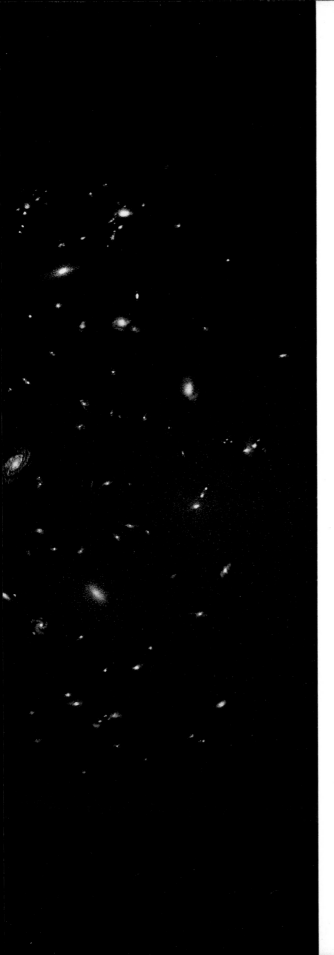

Whispers of the Big Bang

At the time of the Big Bang, all the matter and energy of the Universe was squeezed into one tiny spot! It must have been very hot — trillions of degrees.

But as the Universe expanded, it cooled off. There are still hot spots, like the stars, but overall, the Universe has become much cooler. The light waves of the vast flash of the Big Bang stretched and grew longer as the Universe cooled. Today, they are very long radio waves.

In 1965, those radio waves were detected. Scientists could hear the last faint whisper of the Big Bang of long ago.

This painting shows the history of our expanding Universe. The bright spot on the left represents the Big Bang itself. As you look further to the right, subatomic particles form, then atoms of matter. Next, gas clumps together to form galaxies. Then, within those galaxies, gas further clumps to make stars and planets.

The Early Universe

Light travels at a speed of 186,000 miles (300,000 km) a second. If a star is 10 light-years from us, its light takes 10 years to reach us.

Since the Andromeda Galaxy is over two million light-years from us, its light takes over two million years to reach us! This means that the farther out in <u>space</u> we look, the farther back in <u>time</u> we see!

Light from the most distant known quasar takes about 12 billion years to reach us. Since the Big Bang happened about 15 to 20 billion years ago, we see distant quasars as they looked when the Universe was quite young. In 1988, astronomers announced that they had found objects 17 billion light-years away. They were galaxies being formed when the Universe was still younger. We can't see much farther than that!

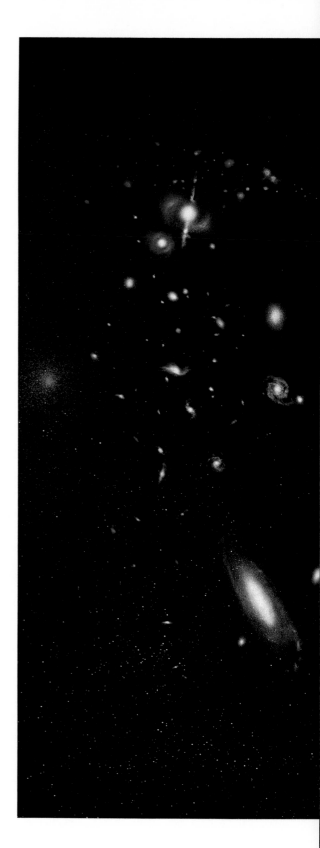

How far is far? The light from our Sun (shown to the upper right of Earth), takes just eight minutes to reach us. Light from the nearest star, Alpha Centauri (the bluish speck shown below Earth), takes 4.2 years. The light we see from the Great Galaxy in Andromeda (the spiral shown lower left) left 2.3 million years ago. And light from the farthest known quasars (upper left) set out 12-15 billion years ago.

How the Universe Changes

Stars stay hot because of nuclear changes in their centers. As a star center grows hotter, the star expands. Eventually, the star explodes and collapses.

When a very large star explodes, it becomes a supernova. Supernovas spread their material through space. In the Big Bang, only the simplest atoms, hydrogen and helium, were formed, but supernovas spread more complex atoms outward.

Our Sun formed from a cloud with these more complex atoms. Almost all the atoms of Earth — and in ourselves — were formed in stars that exploded as supernovas long ago.

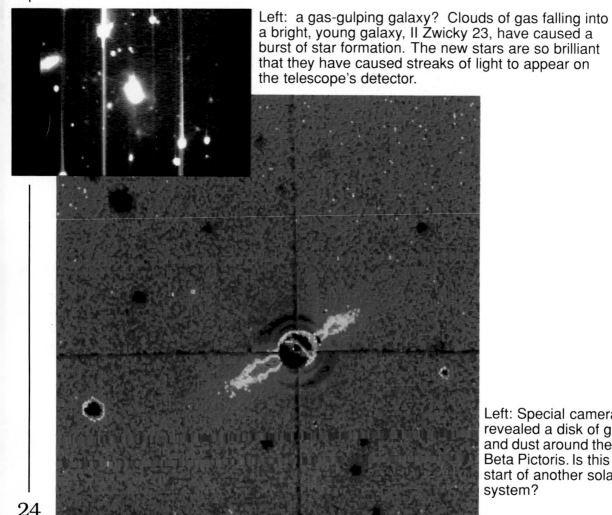

Left: a gas-gulping galaxy? Clouds of gas falling into a bright, young galaxy, II Zwicky 23, have caused a burst of star formation. The new stars are so brilliant that they have caused streaks of light to appear on the telescope's detector.

Left: Special cameras revealed a disk of gas and dust around the star Beta Pictoris. Is this the start of another solar system?

Above: Stars can explode with incredible violence, becoming so bright that they outshine a whole galaxy of normal stars. Supernovas also spread complex elements into space, and the force of the explosions helps stars begin to form.

Left: Galaxy NGC 5128 before (top) and after (bottom) it had a supernova.

A crab in the sky!

In 1054, a supernova only about 5,000 light-years away appeared in the sky. It was brighter than the planet Venus, but a year or so later, it faded away. But what is left of it can still be seen as a small, oddly shaped cloudy patch right where the supernova was. It is a cloud of debris left by the explosion. It's called the Crab Nebula because of its shape. The Crab Nebula has been expanding for almost 1,000 years after the explosion. In its center, there is a tiny neutron star, all that is left of the original giant star that exploded. •

What Will Happen to the Universe?

When a supernova explodes, what is left of it can collapse into a tiny object with gravity so strong that everything falls in, but nothing comes out. This object is called a black hole. There might be a black hole in the center of every galaxy.

The Universe may expand forever, or its own gravity might some day slow its expansion, and even stop it. It might then fall back together in a Big Crunch. And maybe a new Universe will form in a new Big Bang.

Maybe there was a Big Crunch, or even many Big Crunches, before the Big Bang that formed our Universe. We don't know if there ever was. We're still trying to understand the Big Bang that created the present Universe. That's a big enough puzzle for now!

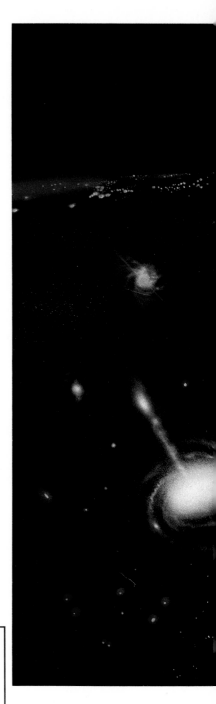

Mini-stars with maxi-mass

When a star explodes and collapses, it becomes incredibly smaller than you might ever expect. It's like breaking up Ping-Pong balls and packing their pieces. Some stars collapse into white dwarf stars. White dwarfs can be smaller than Earth, but they can hold the same amount of matter as the Sun! Even smaller stars, called neutron stars, are formed when very large stars collapse. Neutron stars can be as massive as our Sun, but they might be only a few miles in diameter!

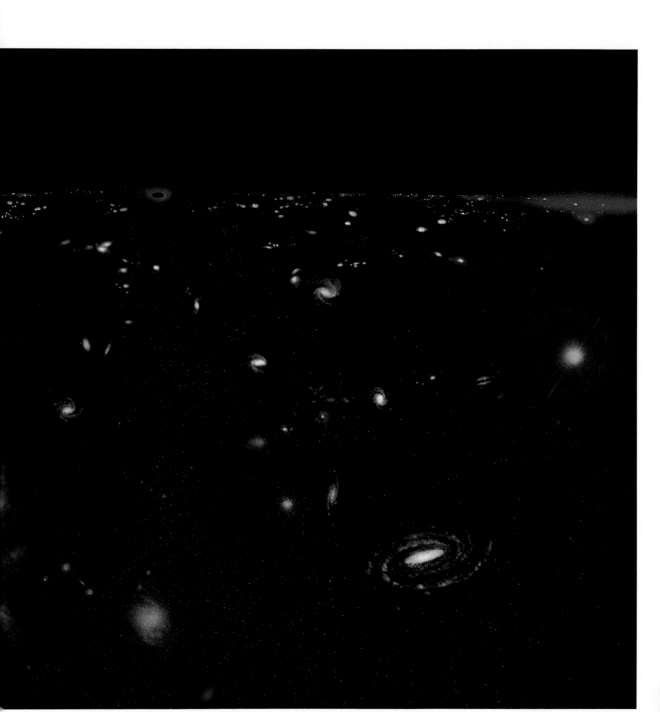

Someday in the very distant future, perhaps the Universe will stop expanding and begin contracting. Everything in the cosmos would fall into an enormous black hole (top of painting) — and perhaps create another Big Bang!

Fact File: Distance and Size in the Universe

We know the Universe is a big place. But just how big is it?

We can talk about the great distances and sizes that exist in the Universe. But maybe the best way to get an idea about just how big those distances and sizes really are is to compare them to distances and sizes we know about and use here on Earth.

Imagine that we could reduce the cosmos to a size we can manage. First let's imagine that we could make the Sun the size of a soccer ball. Then let's shrink the Universe even further, so we could put the entire Solar system in a coffee cup. And finally, let's shrink the entire known Universe down so that all of our Galaxy, the Milky Way, would be no wider than a long-playing record!

Even after reducing the Universe this much, we might be surprised at how far apart everything in the cosmos still seems. We can use the illustration above and the charts on page 29 to get an idea of how big and how far everything is out there — and how much space there is in space.

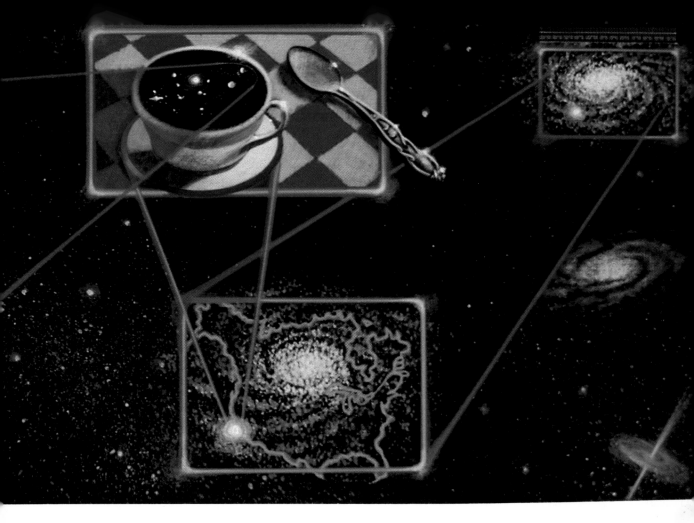

The Sun as a Soccer Ball

What if the Sun was...	Then Earth (our home planet) could be...	And Jupiter (the Solar system's biggest planet) would be...	And Pluto (our Solar system's tiniest known planet) could be...	And Alpha Centauri (the nearest star in our Galaxy) would be...
...a soccer ball about 8 3/4 inches (22 cm) wide?	...a pebble less than 1/10 inch (1/4 cm) wide, and about 78 1/2 feet (24 m) from our soccer-ball Sun.	...a bit bigger than a ball bearing 7/8 inch (2.2 cm) wide.	...a pebble tinier even than Earth, and over 1/2 mile (0.8 km) from our soccer-ball Sun.	...nearly 4 miles (6.4 km) from the soccer-ball Sun at the center of our Solar system.

The Solar System in a Cup

And what if our Solar system was...	Then the Milky Way (our Galaxy) would be...
...small enough to fit in a coffee cup?	...as wide as North America — about 3,000 miles (4,800 km) across!

The Milky Way as a Long-playing Record!

And what if the Milky Way (our Galaxy) was...	Then the Andromeda Galaxy (the galaxy "next door") would be...	And the farthest-known quasars would be...
...a long-playing record about 1 foot (30 cm) wide?	...23 feet (7 m) away from the Milky Way.	...more than 32 miles (51 km) away from the Milky Way!

As big as we think Earth is, it is only a tiny speck in our vast Universe!

More Books About the Universe

Here are more books that contain information about the Universe. If you are interested in them, check your library or bookstore.

Nightwatch: An Equinox Guide to Viewing the Universe. Dickinson (Camden)
Our Milky Way and Other Galaxies. Asimov (Gareth Stevens)
Quasars, Pulsars, and Black Holes. Asimov (Gareth Stevens)
Space & Beyond. Montgomery (Bantam)
The Stars: From Birth to Black Hole. Darling (Dillon)
The Universe. Ciupik (Raintree)
Universe. Zim (Morrow)
Universe: Past, Present & Future. Darling (Dillon)

Places to Visit

You can explore many places in the Universe without leaving Earth. Here are some museums and centers where you can find a variety of space exhibits.

National Museum of Science and Technology
Ottawa, Ontario

Touch the Universe
Manitoba Planetarium
Winnipeg, Manitoba

H. R. MacMillan Planetarium
Vancouver, British Columbia

Henry Crown Space Center
Museum of Science and Industry
Chicago, Illinois

Kansas Cosmosphere and Space Center
Hutchinson, Kansas

American Museum — Hayden Planetarium
New York, New York

Science North Solar Observatory
Sudbury, Ontario

MacDonald Observatory
Austin, Texas

For More Information About the Universe

Here are some places you can write to for more information about the Universe. Be sure to tell them exactly what you want to know about or see. Remember to include your age, full name, and address.

For information about astronomy:
NASA Kennedy Space Center
Educational Services Office
Kennedy Space Center, Florida 32899

Space Communications Branch
Ministry of State for Science and Technology
240 Sparks Street, C. D. Howe Building
Ottawa, Ontario K1A 1A1, Canada

For photographs of stars and galaxies:
Caltech Bookstore
California Institute of Technology
Mail Code 1-51
Pasadena, California 91125

For catalogs of slides, posters, sky maps, and other astronomy material:
AstroMedia Order Dept.
1027 N. 7th Street
Milwaukee, Wisconsin 53233

National Museum of Science and Technology
Astronomy Division
2380 Lancaster Road
Ottawa, Ontario K1A 0M8, Canada

Sky Publishing Corp.
49 Bay State Road
Cambridge, Massachusetts 02238-1290

Glossary

Andromeda Galaxy: the closest spiral galaxy to our own, although it is over 2,000,000 light-years away.

atoms: the smallest particles of elements that can exist. They are the source of nuclear energy when joined together or split apart.

the Big Bang: a gigantic explosion that some scientists believe created our Universe.

billion: in North America — and in this book — the number represented by 1 followed by nine zeroes — 1,000,000,000. In some places, such as the United Kingdom (Britain), this number is called "a thousand million." In these places, one billion would then be represented by 1 followed by *12* zeroes — 1,000,000,000,000: a million million, a number known as a trillion in North America.

black hole: an object in space caused by the explosion and collapse of a star. This object is so tightly packed that not even light can escape the force of its gravity.

Copernicus, Nicolaus: the first modern scholar to suggest, in 1543, that the Sun was at the center of the Universe, with the planets orbiting around it.

Doppler, Christian: the Austrian scientist who, in 1842, showed why noise sounds more shrill when coming toward you, but sounds deeper when moving away from you. Light waves act in a similar way. They are shorter — and appear blue — when they are coming toward you, and become longer — and appear red — when moving away. (See also **red shift**.)

galaxy: any of the billions of large groupings of stars, gas, and dust that exist in the Universe. Our Galaxy is known as the Milky Way Galaxy.

Herschel, William: the German astronomer who, in 1785, showed that the visible stars are all part of a vast collection of stars. He said that our Sun was part of this collection, which today we know as the Milky Way Galaxy.

light-year: the distance that light travels in one year — nearly six trillion miles (9.6 trillion km).

nebula: a cloud of dust and gas in space. Some large nebulas, or nebulae, are the birthplaces of stars. Other nebulae are the debris of dying stars.

neutron stars: very small stars formed when large stars collapse, but which keep much of their very great mass.

optical illusion: something perceived by the eye, a camera, or a telescope that is not what it appears to be. For example, the appearance of a "bridge" of gases from a quasar to a galaxy may be false, a trick played on the "eye" of the telescope — an optical illusion.

quasars: the most distant galaxies in the Universe. They are billions of light-years away from Earth.

radio waves: electromagnetic waves that can be detected by radio receiving equipment.

red shift: the apparent reddening of light given off by an object moving away from us (see **Doppler**). The greater the red shift of light from a distant galaxy, the farther that galaxy is moving away from us.

sphere: a globelike body. The ancient Greeks believed that Earth was a large sphere at the center of the Universe.

supernova: the result of a huge star exploding. When a supernova occurs, material from the star is spread through space.

Universe: everything that we know exists and believe may exist.

variable stars: stars whose brightness changes. Some variable stars change brightness very regularly. Others are unpredictable.

Index

The publishers wish to thank the following for permission to reproduce copyright material: front cover, pp. 17, 19 (both), © Julian Baum, 1988; p. 4 (upper), © Sally Bensusen, 1988; pp. 4 (lower), 8 (upper), 10 (upper), photographs courtesy of Julian Baum; p. 5, © Frank Zullo, 1987; p. 6 (upper), AIP Niels Bohr Library; p. 6 (lower), Mary Evans Picture Library; p. 7, © Anglo-Australian Telescope Board, David Malin, 1980; p. 8 (lower), © George East, 1978; pp. 9, 13, 16, 24 (upper), 25 (lower), National Optical Astronomy Observatories; pp. 10-11, 14-15, © Brian Sullivan, 1988; p. 12, Science Photo Library; pp. 20-21, 22-23, © Paternostro / Schaller, 1988; p. 24 (lower), Jet Propulsion Laboratory; pp. 25 (upper), 26-27, © Mark Paternostro, 1988; pp. 28-29, © Larry Ortiz, 1988.

W9-AJT-056

DATE DUE

DE 27 '89	JY 15 13	
JA 23 '90	JY 10 '08	
MY 29 '90		
DE 26 '90		
MR 2 6 '92		
NOV 30 '92		
JUL 17 '95		
APR 30 '97		
MAY 08 '97		
JUL 28 97		
SEP 29 '99		
JY 17 02		

J
523.1
Asi   Asimov, Isaac
          Mythology and the
          universe

EAU CLAIRE DISTRICT LIBRARY

ISAAC ASIMOV'S
Library of the Universe

Mythology
and the
Universe

EAU CLAIRE DISTRICT LIBRARY

by Isaac Asimov

Gareth Stevens Publishing
Milwaukee

80076

The reproduction rights to all photographs and
illustrations in this book are controlled by the
individuals or institutions credited on page 32 and
may not be reproduced without their permission.

Library of Congress Cataloging-in-Publication Data

Asimov, Isaac, 1920-
    Mythology and the universe / by Isaac Asimov. — A Gareth Stevens
children's book ed.
            p.   cm. — (Isaac Asimov's library of the universe)
    Bibliography: p.
    Includes index.
    Summary: Presents some ancient mythological beliefs about the universe.
    ISBN 1-55532-403-7
    1. Astronomy—Juvenile literature.   2. Cosmology—Juvenile literature.
[1. Astronomy—Folklore.] I. Title. II. Series: Asimov, Isaac, 1920-   Library of
the universe.
QB46.A785   1989
523.1—dc20   89-11360

A Gareth Stevens Children's Books edition
Edited, designed, and produced by
Gareth Stevens, Inc.
RiverCenter Building, Suite 201
1555 North RiverCenter Drive
Milwaukee, Wisconsin 53212, USA

Text copyright © 1990 by Nightfall, Inc.
End matter copyright © 1990 by Gareth Stevens, Inc.
Format copyright © 1990 by Gareth Stevens, Inc.

First published in the United States and Canada in 1990 by Gareth Stevens, Inc.
All rights reserved. No part of this book may be reproduced or used in any form
or by any means without permission in writing from Gareth Stevens, Inc.

**For a free color catalog describing Gareth Stevens' list of high-quality children's
books call 1-800-341-3569.**

Cover design by Matthew Groshek and Kate Kriege, © Gareth Stevens, Inc.

Project editor: Mark Sachner
Editor: Rhoda Irene Sherwood
Series design: Laurie Shock
Book design: Kate Kriege
Research editor: Kathleen Weisfeld Barrilleaux
Picture research: Matthew Groshek
Technical advisers and consulting editors: Julian Baum and Francis Reddy

Printed in the United States of America

1 2 3 4 5 6 7 8 9 95 94 93 92 91 90

CONTENTS

Nowadays, we have seen planets up close, all the way to distant Uranus and Neptune. We have mapped Venus through its clouds. We have seen dead volcanoes on Mars and live ones on Io, one of Jupiter's satellites. We have detected strange objects no one knew anything about till recently: quasars, pulsars, black holes. We have studied stars not only by the light they give out but by other kinds of radiation: infrared, ultraviolet, x-rays, radio waves. We have even detected tiny particles called neutrinos that are given off by the stars.

But in ancient times, people could look at the sky with nothing but their eyes — and could only wonder about what they saw. They created stories about what they saw. Some of the stories they created helped them make sense out of the objects in the sky. Others were just dramatic inventions of the human imagination. And many of them influence us to this day.

Isaac Asimov

Different peoples had different images of the Sun: a Sun being as drawn in Europe in the Middle Ages (above); a dragon below the fiery Sun, from 18th-century China (right); the great eye of Ra, Sun god of the ancient Egyptians (below).

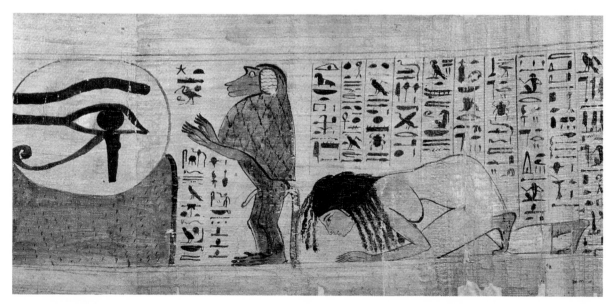

Earth's Providers — The Sun . . .

The Sun gives light and warmth. Near Earth's Equator, the Sun remains high in the sky. But farther north or south, the Sun is sometimes low in the sky. When this happens, the days become shorter and cooler, and winter comes. Winter is a reminder that without the Sun, there would be only darkness and freezing cold, so the ancients pictured the Sun as a glorious and good god.

The Greeks thought of the Sun god, Helios (or Apollo), as driving a flaming chariot across the sky. The Babylonians said the Sun god, Shamash, gave laws to people. The Egyptian Sun god, Ra, was considered the nation's protector. One king of Egypt, Akhenaton (pronounced AH-kuh-NAH-tin), thought the Sun god, whom he called Aton, was the <u>only</u> god. This king was the first person we know of to believe in only one god.

As summer approaches at the Arctic or Antarctic circles, the Sun travels a growing arc through the sky — and there are eventually days when it never sets!

The brightest star — bringing "dog days" to Earth?

The sky's brightest star, Sirius, is in the constellation of Canis Major ("Great Dog"). Canis Major is near the constellation of Orion (the Hunter), so it is said to be the Hunter's dog. Ancient Greeks thought Sirius was so bright that it must deliver heat to Earth like a little Sun. And when Sirius and our Sun were in the sky together, they supposedly gave Earth its midsummer heat. This is not so, but we do call this hot period the "dog days."

. . . And the Moon

The Moon is much dimmer than the Sun, but its light at night is cool and helpful. In myths, the Moon is usually pictured as a gentle female. To the Greeks, she was Selene or Artemis. To the Egyptians, she was Isis.

Left: This "moon monster" was drawn on a shield used by a Crow Indian.

The Moon changes its appearance, going through a cycle from thin crescent to full and back to crescent each month. Ancient calendars were based on this monthly cycle, and 12 of these monthly cycles made up the cycle of the season. It thus became very important to watch each month for the first sign of the "new Moon." In fact, both "month" and "Monday" come from the word "moon."

Right, above: The ancient Greeks pictured the Moon as a beautiful maiden, Selene, riding a silver chariot.

Right: A Moonwatch? Sure! This special clock is designed to show the phases of the Moon.

For as long as people have gazed at the Moon they have imagined pictures on its face. The "Man in the Moon" (below, opposite) is probably the most common picture. Others include the Rabbit (below) and the Maiden (below, right).

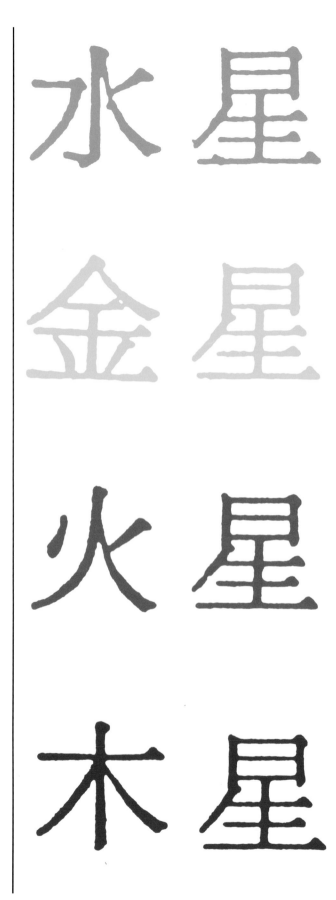

The Ancient Planets

From day to day and from night to night, the Sun and Moon change their positions against the stars in the sky. So do the five bright starlike objects that we call "planets" (from the Greek word for "wanderers"). The ancient Babylonians watched the planets move across the sky and gave them the names of gods. The Greeks and Romans copied the Babylonians in this, and we use the Roman names to this day.

The brightest planet in the sky is Venus, named for the goddess of beauty. A red planet the color of blood is Mars, named after the god of war. The fastest-moving planet is Mercury, named after the messenger of the gods, and the slowest planet known in ancient times is Saturn, named for the god of agriculture. The second brightest planet in the sky, Jupiter, was named for the chief god. Jupiter is not as bright as Venus, but it shines all night, while Venus appears only in the evening or at dawn.

Ancient Chinese names of the four brightest planets. From the top row: "Water Star" (Mercury); "Gold Star" (Venus); "Fire Star" (Mars); "Wood Star" (Jupiter).

8

Left: Mercury, the quick-footed messenger of the gods.

Below: Astrologers claim that each planet most influences people born under certain astrological signs. Here Venus, the goddess of love, is pictured on her chariot. The signs she rules, Taurus and Libra, make up the wheels of the cart.

Left: In Greek myth, Charon ferried the souls of the dead across the River Styx and into the underworld of Pluto. In 1978, when astronomers found a moon orbiting the planet Pluto, the name Charon fit the newly discovered world perfectly.

Bottom: Percival Lowell, the astronomer who mounted the search for a planet beyond Neptune.

Right: a modern cartoon character who seems delighted to be answering to the name of Pluto.

The Modern Planets

In modern times, people have found new planets that are too far away for the ancients to have seen. These planets have been given names from mythology, too.

Beyond Saturn is Uranus, named for the god of the sky, who was Saturn's father. Farther still is Neptune, a sea green planet named for the god of the sea. Beyond Neptune is Pluto, named for the god of the underworld because it is so far from the light of the Sun.

Satellites and asteroids are also named for mythological figures. For example, Neptune's satellite is named for the god's son, Triton. In 1801, the first asteroid in the asteroid belt between Mars and Jupiter was discovered. It was named Ceres, after the goddess of agriculture. Other satellites and asteroids, such as Charon (Pluto's tiny moon), Leda and Io (both moons of Jupiter), Atlas, Prometheus, and Phoebe (moons of Saturn), and Juno, Eros, and Pallas (asteroids) are also named after mythological figures.

Okay, kids — name that planet!

In 1930, a new observatory finally enabled astronomers to see Pluto. They realized that Pluto is so far from the Sun that it receives only dim light. For this reason, an 11-year-old English schoolgirl thought this "new" planet should be named after Pluto, god of the underworld, where everything is dim. Also, PL, the first letters of Pluto, are the initials of Percival Lowell, the man who built the observatory from which Pluto was first seen.

11

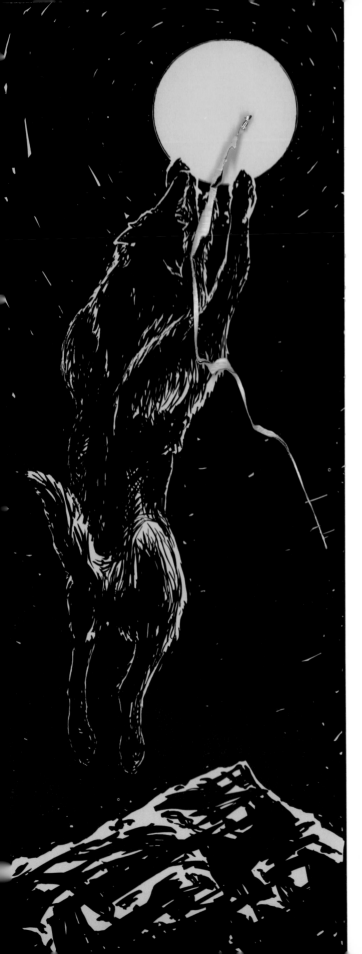

Eclipse — The Death of the Moon and Sun?

Every so often, something unusual happens in the sky: The Sun or Moon is eclipsed and hidden from our view. The Sun is eclipsed because the Moon moves in front of it and hides its light. The Moon is eclipsed because it moves into Earth's shadow.

Ancient people didn't know these causes, so they invented causes of their own. Some thought the Sun and Moon were chased by wolves, dragons, or other monsters that caught up with them now and then and started to swallow them. People would then shout and bang drums to scare away the monsters and bring back the Sun and Moon.

Of course, the Sun and Moon always <u>have</u> come back from their eclipses. And they will continue to do so for billions of years, even though according to Norse myths, a giant wolf <u>will</u> finally swallow the Sun at the world's end.

According to Norse myths, giant wolves will catch the Sun and Moon at the end of the world.

Meteors — a big hit in everyone's book

Every once in a while, we see a "shooting star." Some people think "shooting stars" fall, but they are really meteoroids streaking through the air as blazing meteors, and, in some cases, reaching Earth as meteorites. Throughout history, people have thought meteorites were holy objects. For instance, the Black Stone in the Kaaba, which Muslims consider holy, is probably a meteorite. But scientists aren't allowed to study it, so no one really knows.

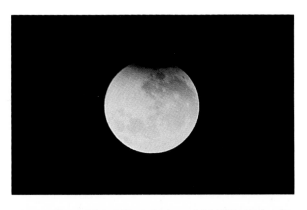

During a lunar eclipse, the Moon's bright face turns a dusky red as it slips into Earth's shadow.

In one Hindu story, the dragon Rahu causes an eclipse whenever he catches the Sun or Moon.

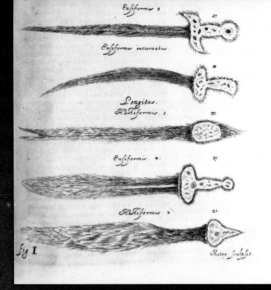

Comet tails —
more bark than bite

Comet tails contain poison gases but are so thin that the poison in them can't hurt anyone. In 1910, Earth was about to pass through the tail of Halley's Comet. Astronomers assured people nothing would happen, but many folks panicked anyway, thinking they would be poisoned and die. Some scoundrels sold phony pills, telling people they would prevent poisoning. Of course, no one was poisoned on May 16, 1910 — at least not by Earth's passing through Halley's tail.

Comets — The Hairy Stars

Comets appear in the sky now and then. They are hazy objects with long tails. With a little imagination, they might look like the heads of mourning women with long, streaming hair — and in fact, the word "comet" comes from the Greek word for "hair."

Sometimes comets look like swords, so people had several reasons to think of them as unpleasant omens. It's no wonder, then, that most people thought comets were messages sent by the gods, warning of war, plague, and destruction. People would pray or ring church bells in order to try to ward off the evil. But evil always came when there were comets in the sky.

Of course, evil always came when comets were <u>not</u> in the sky, too — but people somehow didn't notice that!

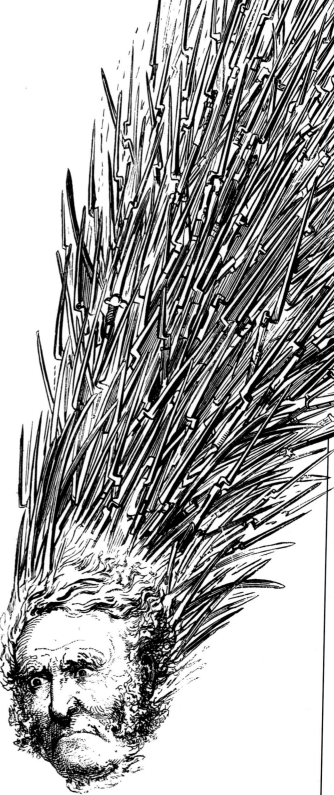

Opposite: Comet West blazed through the winter skies of 1976. Inset: Comets were often considered bad news. People often pictured them as swordlike omens of war or disaster.

Above: The "Great War Comet" of 1861 bears a resemblance to Jefferson Davis, president of the Confederate States of America — a celestial warning of the US Civil War?

EAU CLAIRE DISTRICT LIBRARY

Above, left: To the ancient Japanese, the two brightest stars of Orion represented two samurai warriors. Separated by the constellation's central three stars, they are about to engage in combat. Above, right: While we see Orion's central trio of stars as the hunter's belt, the Japanese see an entirely different constellation. It represents a special cup from which people sip wine to celebrate the New Year.

**Our Milky Way —
the ultimate constellation?**

Stretching across the sky is a foggy band of light, the Milky Way. Early Sumerians, medieval Vikings, and American Indians saw it as a bridge between Earth and the sky for the dead to walk on. Other ancients thought it was a stream of milk from a goddess feeding her baby. An ancient Greek, Democritus, said it was actually a band of stars so dim and numerous that they just <u>looked</u> like a fog of light. He was right, but how did he know when no one else did? **?**

Stars Together — Constellations

When you look at the stars, you may imagine that they form patterns. Some of these patterns are squares. Some are shaped like a "W." Some form wiggly lines. Two bright stars might be close together and appear to be related when viewed from Earth.

Ancient people imagined many shapes in the sky, including even people and animals. These shapes made it easier to locate the stars. A star might be in the "tail of the scorpion" or in the "head of the hunter." These patterns are called "constellations," a word that comes from two Latin words which basically mean "stars together." The constellations were given names, many of them in Latin. We thus speak of "Ursa Major" for the "Great Bear." The ancients also created stories about these imaginary figures in the sky.

The traditional view of the constellation Orion is based on a Greek myth about a great hunter (opposite, lower right).

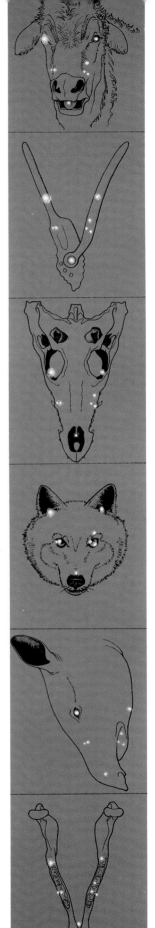

bull's head
the Greek and Roman constellation Taurus

nutcracker
(Indonesia)

crocodile's skull
(New Guinea)

wolf's head
(Germany)

tapir's head
(South America)

bull's jaw
(Babylonia)

A 13th-century artist pictures the month of May. In the blue arc at the top of the painting, the Sun moves from the constellation Taurus (the Bull) into Gemini (the Twins). Venus, the love goddess, watches over the people on Earth from her blue chariot (top, center).

Sky Wanderers — The Zodiac

The Sun, Moon, and planets each move in a large circle all around the sky. All of these objects pass through the same constellations as they make their circle. The ancients divided this circle into 12 constellations, so that the Sun took one month to go through each one. They pictured most of the constellations as animals, so the band in which the planets move is known as the "zodiac," which means "circle of animals." Thanks in large part to the zodiac, the number 12 became important both in mythology and as the basis for our calendar.

Many experts believe that the signs of the zodiac began nearly 4,000 years ago in the Middle East with the Babylonians. From the Babylonians, the zodiac passed on to the ancient Greeks, Egyptians, and Chinese. The Aztec Indians also created a system similar to the zodiac. Most experts believe that they did this independently of the Babylonians.

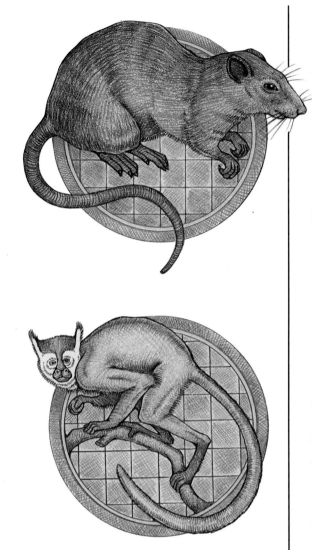

Top to bottom: the Rat, Monkey, and Rooster — three animals from the Japanese zodiac.

19

New Constellations

Some constellations in the Northern Hemisphere never set. One of these, Ursa Major (Great Bear), contains the Big Dipper, which points to the North Star, Polaris. Sailors in old times noticed that Ursa Major was always in the northern sky. So they could look for it and always tell which direction was north. Thanks to the Dipper, sailors could voyage far from land and find their way home.

Some constellations never rise in the north and can only be seen from the Southern Hemisphere. Modern scientists worked out names for these southern constellations. They used images that weren't mythological, giving them Latin names meaning things like "easel," "compasses," and "microscope," and even "air pump."

Opposite: As Western sailors viewed the strange skies of the Southern Hemisphere, they made up new constellations — such as Horologium (the Clock).

With the help of a device called a sextant and a little math, sailors can find their position on the Earth by observing the positions of the Sun and stars.

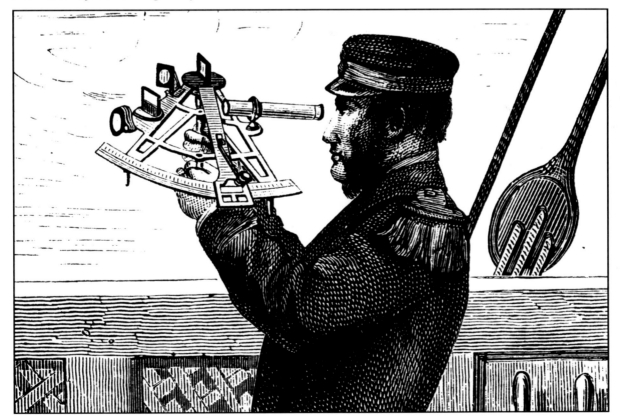

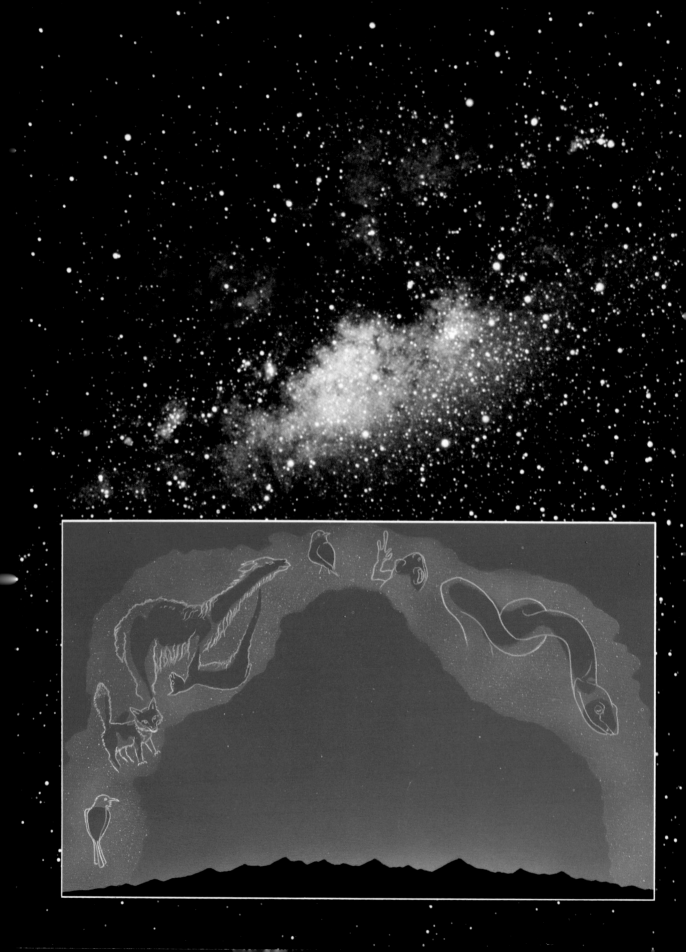

Constellations — Different Things to Different People

We know that both ancient and modern cultures have seen figures in the constellations. Sometimes these figures are remarkably similar. Babylonians as well as ancient Mongols saw the Milky Way as a seam sewn in the two halves of heaven. And as you learned earlier in this book, several cultures from different times and places — the Sumerians, Vikings, and some American Indians — believed the Milky Way was a bridge between Earth and the sky for the dead.

But most cultures differ in their reading of the stars. When 18th-century Mongols looked at Ursa Major, they saw not the Great Bear, but seven old men. Some American Indian children learned that the Milky Way was the two protective hands of Father Sky. The Inca Indians had an even more unusual reading of the skies. They interpreted the dark clouds of the Milky Way, rather than the stars, and saw in them animals such as a bird, fox, llama, toad, and serpent.

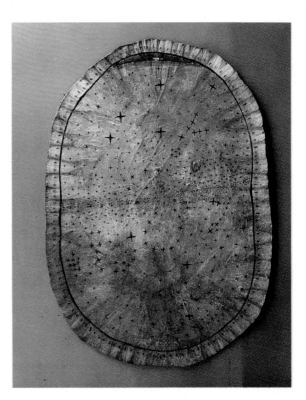

Opposite, background: Dark stretches of dust wind through the Milky Way, a faint, broad band of light that runs across the night sky. Inset: The Incas of South America formed constellations out of the Milky Way's dark stretches of dust.

Right: A star map sketched on a piece of deerskin used by the Skidi Pawnee Indians. The stars of many other constellations, such as the Big and Little Dippers, are also visible.

The Pole Stars

To the Norse, it was a huge spike driven through the Universe around which the heavens revolved. To the Mongols, it was the Golden Peg, a stake that kept the heavens from whirling apart. The Chinese likened it to an emperor, the chief star that ruled the others. In India, it was the place where a holy young prince faithfully meditated. "It" was the Pole Star, that stable star in the north that has guided travelers for thousands of years.

But there is no one Pole Star. Instead, because our planet's axis wobbles just a bit, Earth shifts in its journey through the skies over thousands of years. So various stars have been the Pole Star: Alderamin, Deneb, Vega, Thuban, and our current Pole Star, Polaris. And, of course, during those years, there have been periods when there was no star exactly to the north.

Background, opposite: Stars arc across the sky in this long-exposure photograph. The stars closest to Polaris, the North Star, don't move much at all. Inset: The two stars at the end of the Big Dipper's bowl (right) point toward the North Star.

The Demon Star — look if you dare

Perseus, a hero in Greek mythology, killed Medusa, a monster with snakes in her hair. According to the myths, people turned to stone just by looking at her. The constellation Perseus holds the head of Medusa. One bright star stands out in her "head." Instead of shining steadily, it slowly brightens and dims. The ancients hardly mentioned it but must have noticed it and felt uneasy. They called it the Demon Star. The Arabs named it Algol ("the Ghoul"), which is its name today.

ASTROSCOPE

Your Daily Horoscope

Advice from the stars for Friday, Nov. 10, 1989

Aquarius (those born Jan. 20-Feb. 19) Look for and talk with those who share your interests. You may have more in common with others than you think!

Pisces (Feb. 20-March 20) Be suspicious of people who appear to share your interests. They may just be trying to take advantage of you.

Aries (March 21-April 19) Don't be discouraged by mistakes you make today. With a little patience, everything will work out fine.

Taurus (April 20-May 20) People may say nice things to you — and about you — today. Listen to them carefully. Their advice could be quite valuable.

Gemini (May 21-June 20) People may say nice things about you today. Don't be so trusting! Be careful of their advice.

Cancer (June 21-July 22) Make plans for that long automobile trip you've been thinking about.

Leo (July 23-Aug. 22) This is not your lucky day. Stay away from machines!

Virgo (Aug. 23-Sept. 22) Someone may give you a chance to spend a sizable sum of money today. Be cautious and think it over before taking the plunge.

Libra (Sept. 23-Oct. 23) There are people less fortunate than you. Today you will know where to find them. Do what you can for them.

Scorpio (Oct. 24-Nov. 22) A good day to be with friends. Find as many as you can with birthdays close to yours and celebrate them together.

Sagittarius (Nov. 23-Dec. 21) Don't confuse people by rushing about. Good stay-at-home day. Bake something sweet with someone you love.

Capricorn (Dec. 22-Jan. 19) Be on the move. Don't stay in one place for too long. Today is your day to keep people guessing!

Modern Myths

People tell stories about the objects in the sky in different ways. Astronomers talk about the skies in ways that we have become familiar with. Other people called astrologers talk about the skies in ways that are less familiar. Their practice, dating from ancient times, is to work out methods for predicting the future by using the position of the planets in the zodiac. This practice is called astrology.

Scientists are skeptical about astrology, but many people believe it to be true, just as ancient peoples found <u>their</u> stories of the skies to be true. So history shows us that while we are still uncovering secrets about the Universe, one thing remains certain: our endless desire to make sense out of the objects above and around us.

Opposite: Astrologers claim — with little evidence — that the stars and planets affect our moods and fortunes. Even today, many major newspapers carry a "horoscope" for those who seek advice from the stars.

The 13-ft (4-m) telescope of Kitt Peak National Observatory peers into the skies for answers to our questions about the cosmos.

Fact File: Faded Constellations

Sometimes it's hard to imagine just what ancient star-gazers had in mind when they decided to name the star patterns visible from Earth. For example, did the Greeks really see the figure of the mythological hunter Orion in a constellation that looks more like the figure of an hourglass (see pages 16-17)? The fact is that people name things for many reasons. If a group of stars reminds us of a telescope, we might name it after a telescope. But sometimes we name things to honor our myths and legends, or to honor certain objects, events, or people both real and mythological — like Orion. After all, areas of land on Earth are named for similar reasons. And wouldn't it be silly to expect the boundaries of a city or state called Washington to look like a profile of George Washington?

There are also many reasons why the names, shapes, and legends of certain constellations have disappeared. Sometimes, over the course of centuries, the stars shift enough to move out of old patterns and into new ones. Sometimes a rich and thriving culture, like that of the American Indians, is conquered or disappears. Sometimes later generations simply choose to ignore a name that seems too sentimental, like the name of a favorite pet or instrument. Sometimes, the constellation does not disappear but is merely renamed, like Andromeda.

None of the constellation names in the chart or pictures on these pages is used any longer. But they remind us of one thing about human nature that will never change — our urge to observe the Universe, give it meaning, and name as much of it as we can.

Constellations That Came and Went

NAME	COMMENTS
Tiamat	Named by the Babylonians to represent the Great Mother who was murdered by her grandson for plotting to overthrow the gods. Like many constellations, Tiamat was "borrowed" from the Babylonians by the ancient Greeks, and today it is known as Andromeda, whose story is about her rescue from a sea monster named Cetus (another constellation) by the Greek hero Perseus (also one of the constellations).
Mons Maenalus	Named in 1679 for the mountain home of the Greek god Pan.
Bufo (the Toad)	Named in 1768 by John Hill, an eccentric English physician; composed out of a noticeable cluster of stars near the constellations Scorpio and Libra.
Limax (the Slug)	Also named in 1768 by John Hill. The constellation represents a snail without its shell. Most of the stars in this extinct constellation are toward the head and lower parts of the body, with few in the middle.

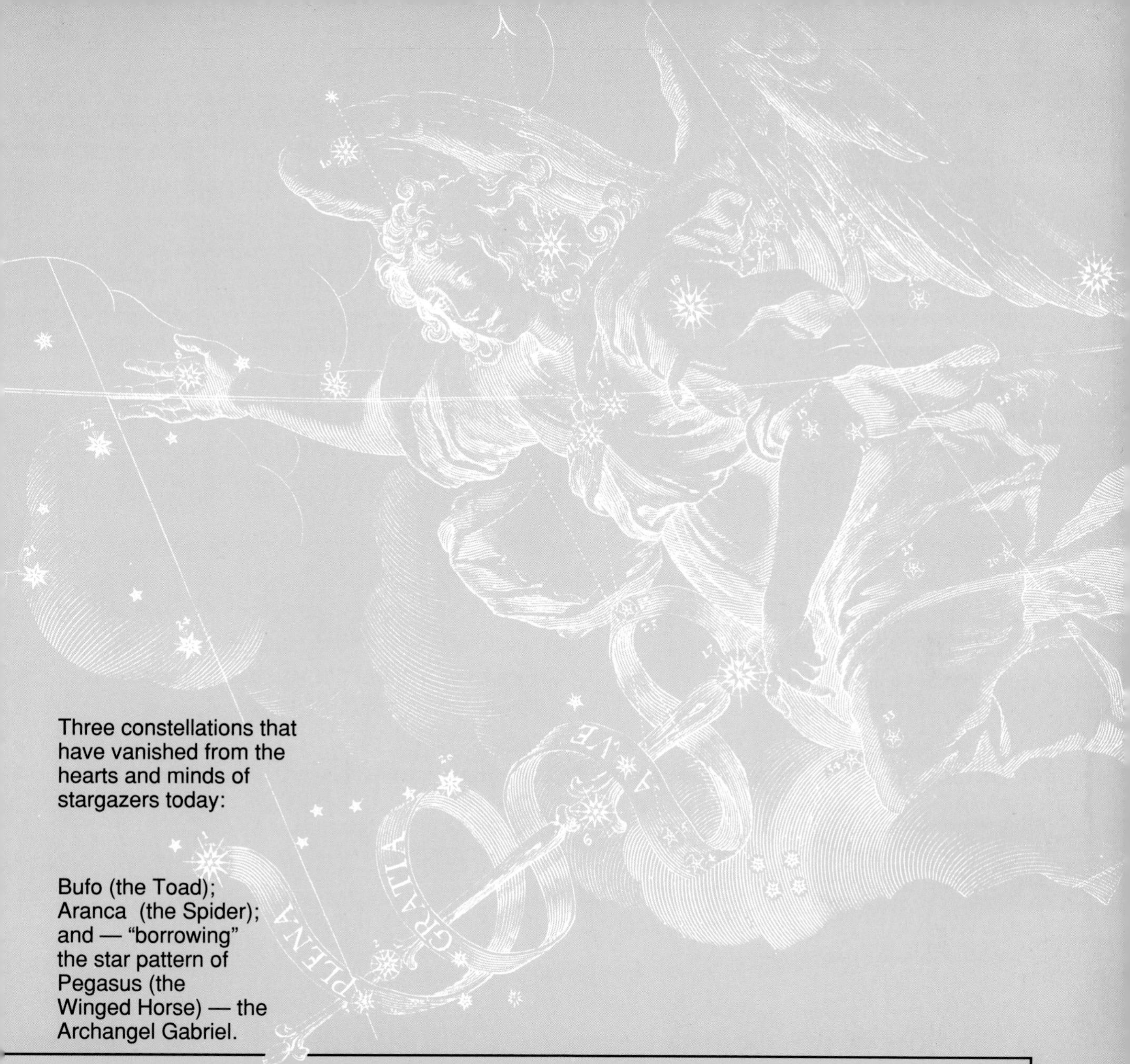

Three constellations that have vanished from the hearts and minds of stargazers today:

Bufo (the Toad); Aranca (the Spider); and — "borrowing" the star pattern of Pegasus (the Winged Horse) — the Archangel Gabriel.

NAME	COMMENTS
Felis (the Cat)	Was named in 1799 by J. J. L. de Lalande, a person who simply liked cats. The name has not been used since the 19th century.
Officina Typographica (the Printing Office)	A constellation visible in the Southern Hemisphere. Was named in 1799 to honor the invention of the printing press.
Telescopium Herschel II	Named in 1781 to honor the German-born English astronomer who discovered Uranus.
Circle of Chiefs	Represents Tirawahat, the central force of the Universe. Named by the Skidi Pawnee Indians, who once arranged their villages in patterns that duplicated the positions of their most important star gods in the sky.
Seven Boys Transformed into Geese	Named by the Chumash Indians of California. This constellation is now known in North America as the Big Dipper.

More Books About Mythology and the Universe

Here are more books about mythology and space. If you are interested in them, check your library or bookstore.

Astro-Dome Book: 3-D Map of the Night Sky. Hunig (Constellation)
Discovering the Stars. Santrey (Troll)
Find the Constellations. Rey (Houghton Mifflin)
Night Sky. Barrett (Franklin Watts)
Outer Space. Jobes (Scarecrow)
The Space Spotter's Guide. Asimov (Gareth Stevens)
Words from the Myths. Asimov (New American Library)

Places to Visit

You can roam among the constellations without leaving Earth. Here are some museums, observatories, and planetariums where you can ponder the cosmos to your heart's content.

Cormack Planetarium
Providence, Rhode Island

David Dunlap Observatory
Richmond Hill, Ontario

Centennial Planetarium
Calgary, Alberta

Burke-Gaffney Planetarium
Halifax, Nova Scotia

Rauch Memorial Planetarium
Louisville, Kentucky

Sunrise Children's Museum Planetarium
Charleston, West Virginia

For More Information About Mythology and the Universe

Here are some people you can write to or call for more information about constellations. Be sure to tell them exactly what you want to know about. And include your full name and address so they can write back to you.

Astronomical "Hotline" for up-to-date descriptions of the sky:
Dial (416) 586-5751
The McLaughlin Planetarium
Toronto, Ontario

For monthly sky maps:
National Museum of Science and Technology
Astronomy Division
P.O. Box 9724, Ottawa Terminal
Ottawa, Ontario K1G 5A3, Canada

For catalogs of slides, posters, and other astronomy materials:
AstroMedia Order Department
21027 Crossroads Circle
Waukesha, Wisconsin 53187

Selectory Sales
Astronomical Society of the Pacific
1290 24th Avenue
San Francisco, California 94122

Sky Publishing Corporation
49 Bay State Road
Cambridge, Massachusetts 02238-1290

Hansen Planetarium
15 South State Street
Salt Lake City, Utah 84111

Glossary

asteroid: "star-like." The asteroids are very small planets made of rock or metal. There are thousands of them in our Solar system, and they mainly orbit the Sun in large numbers between Mars and Jupiter. But some show up elsewhere in the Solar system — some as meteoroids and some possibly as "captured" moons of planets such as Mars.

astrology: the study of the positions of the stars and planets and their supposed influence upon humans and events on Earth.

astronomer: a person involved in the scientific study of the Universe and its various bodies.

calendar: a system for dividing time, most commonly into days, weeks, and months. Every calendar has a starting day and ending day for the year.

Ceres: the Roman goddess of agriculture; the first asteroid to be discovered (1801).

chariot: a two-wheeled horse-drawn car used in ancient times for battles, processions, and races.

comet: an object made of ice, rock, and gas; has a vapor tail that may be seen when the comet's orbit brings it close to the Sun.

constellation: a grouping of stars in the sky that seems to trace out a familiar figure or symbol. Constellations are named after that which they are thought to resemble.

"dog days": the period between early July and early September when the hot weather of summer usually occurs in the Northern Hemisphere.

eclipse: the partial or complete blocking of light from one astronomical body by another.

Halley's Comet: comet that passes by Earth on an average of every 76.1 years. Named for English astronomer Edmund Halley, it is notable in that every pass by this comet has been documented since its first recorded sighting by the Chinese in 240 BC. Its last pass occurred in 1986.

meteor: a meteoroid that has entered Earth's atmosphere. Also, the bright streak of light made as the meteoroid enters or moves through the atmosphere.

meteorite: a meteoroid when it hits Earth.

meteoroid: a lump of rock or metal drifting through space. Meteoroids can be as big as asteroids or as small as specks of dust.

Milky Way: the name of our Galaxy.

mythology: the traditional stories about the gods and legendary heroes of a group of people.

"new Moon": crescent-shaped bit of the Moon's lighter side we see as the Moon begins a new cycle; also, the phase when the Moon is invisible to us.

Pluto: the farthest known planet in our Solar system and one so small that some believe it to be a large asteroid.

satellite: a smaller body orbiting a larger body. The Moon is Earth's <u>natural</u> satellite. Sputnik 1 and 2 were Earth's first <u>artificial</u> satellites.

shooting star: a meteor appearing as a temporary streak of light in the night sky.

underworld: in Greek mythology, the place where it was believed people went when they died.

Ursa Major: "Great Bear"; a constellation near the North Star containing the stars that form the Big Dipper.

zodiac: the band of constellations across the sky that represents the paths of the Sun, the Moon, Mercury, Venus, Mars, Jupiter, and Saturn.

Index

The publishers wish to thank the following for permission to reproduce copyright and other material: front cover, design by Matthew Groshek and Kate Kriege/© Gareth Stevens, Inc., 1989; p. 4 (upper left), copyright-free reproduction from Ridley's *A Short Treatise of Magnetic Bodies and Motions*; pp. 4 (center and bottom), 7 (top), Michael Holford; pp. 5, 6, 8, 11, 12, 13, 15, 17, 19, 21, 23, 25, 27, 28 (postage stamps), from the collection of George G. Young, Astronomy Study Unit of the American Topical Association; p. 5, © Forrest Baldwin; p. 6, copyright-free reproduction of a Crow Indian shield, *ca.* 1804; pp. 7 (center), 26 (left), photographs by Matthew Groshek/© Gareth Stevens, Inc., 1989; pp. 6 (lower right), 7 (bottom, both), 12 (left), 13 (bottom), 16 (upper, both), Rick Karpinski/DeWalt and Associates, 1989; pp. 9 (upper), 11 (lower), 16 (lower), © Keith Ward, 1989; p. 9 (lower), Yerkes Observatory photograph; pp. 10 (upper left), 21 (lower), Mary Evans Picture Library; p. 10 (center), Photofest; p. 10 (lower right), Lowell Observatory photograph; p. 13 (center), © Matthew Groshek, 1986; p. 14 (full page), © John Laborde, 1976; pp. 14 (inset), 28-29 (all), courtesy of the Adler Planetarium, Chicago; p. 15 (right), Historical Pictures Service, Chicago; p. 17 (right, all), © Sally Bensusen, 1989; p. 18, Giraudon/Art Resource, New York; p. 19 (right, all), © Matthew Powell, 1989; p. 20, © Gareth Stevens, Inc., 1989; pp. 22 (full page), 24 (full page), 27 (lower), National Optical Astronomy Observatories; p. 22 (inset), © Sally Bensusen; p. 23 (lower), Field Museum of Natural History, #16231c; p. 24 (inset), © H. M. Heyn, 1988; p. 25 (right), the University of Chicago Library; p. 26 (right), Ann Ronan Picture Library.

EAU CLAIRE DISTRICT LIBRARY